How to Raise BUTTERFLIES

How to Raise BUTTERFLIES

E. Jaediker Norsgaard

Color photographs by

Campbell Norsgaard

G. P. PUTNAM'S SONS
New York

Published in 1990 by G. P. Putnam's Sons, a division of
The Putnam & Grosset Book Group, 200 Madison Avenue,
New York, New York 10016. Originally published in 1988
by Dodd, Mead & Company, Inc. Published simultaneously
in Canada. Printed in the United States of America.
Book design by Jean Krulis.

Library of Congress Cataloging-in-Publication Data Norsgaard, E. Jaediker (Ernestine Jaediker) How to raise butterflies. Reprint. Originally Published: New York: Dodd, Mead, © 1988. SUMMARY: Explains the life cycle of the monarch butterfly through detailed instructions on how to raise that species and other kinds of butterflies. 1. Butterfly farming—Juvenile literature. 2. Butterflies—Juvenile literature. 3. Monarch butterfly—Juvenile literature. [1. Butterfly farming. 2. Monarch butterfly. 3. Butterflies. I. Norsgaard, Cambell, ill. II. Title.] [SF562.B8N67 1990]
638'.5789 90-8056 ISBN 0-339-61286 6
3 5 7 9 10 8 6 4 2

For you, with love

A Skipper sipping nectar

One of the joys of summer is watching butterflies fluttering around flowers in meadows and gardens. Some butterflies are brightly colored and have spots, speckles, or stripes on their wings. As they drink the sweet juice or nectar of the flowers, they seem more like flying flowers themselves than like insects.

A tiny Crescent butterfly enlarged so that you can see its scales

Butterflies are classified as Lepidoptera, which means scale-winged. The scales give their wings an appearance of velvet and rub off like fine dust if touched.

Lepidoptera

Butterflies don't start out in life with wings but must work their way through four stages: egg, caterpillar (larval stage), chrysalis (pupal stage), and winged adult. This process is called *metamorphosis,* a Greek word that means "change of form."

It is an amazing process to watch, and you can do that by raising a butterfly yourself. And then you can have the satisfaction of releasing your butterfly to pollinate flowers. Butterflies are valuable pollinators, as we shall see.

A Monarch caterpillar, chrysalis, and butterfly

RAISING A MONARCH BUTTERFLY

Monarch butterflies are well known in many parts of the world because milkweed, eaten by their young, grows in so many places. You can recognize Monarchs by their orange wings veined in black, with black margins decorated by two rows of white dots.

Trying to get an extra-close look at a Monarch

Monarchs are among the few migrating butterflies, flying incredible distances. In autumn they migrate from eastern and central United States and southeastern Canada to winter in central Mexico. There, they rest on trees by the hundreds of thousands. As winter ends, they mate, fertilizing the females' eggs.

Then, flying northward, Monarchs arrive in the southern states in spring. Most of those reaching the northern states by summer are females that have been laying eggs along the way. (Some of their offspring reach up into Canada—the southern parts of Ontario and Quebec, and all of New Brunswick and Nova Scotia.) Almost all males die on the way north from the wintering grounds.

Western Monarchs are found in greatest numbers west of the Rocky Mountains. They winter in California, along the coast from Monterey to Los Angeles.

THE EGG HUNT

The first step in raising Monarchs is to find their eggs. For that, you must look for milkweed plants growing in meadows, weed-filled lots, or along roadsides. You may see a female Monarch searching too, since milkweed leaves are the only food her young will eat.

Milkweed

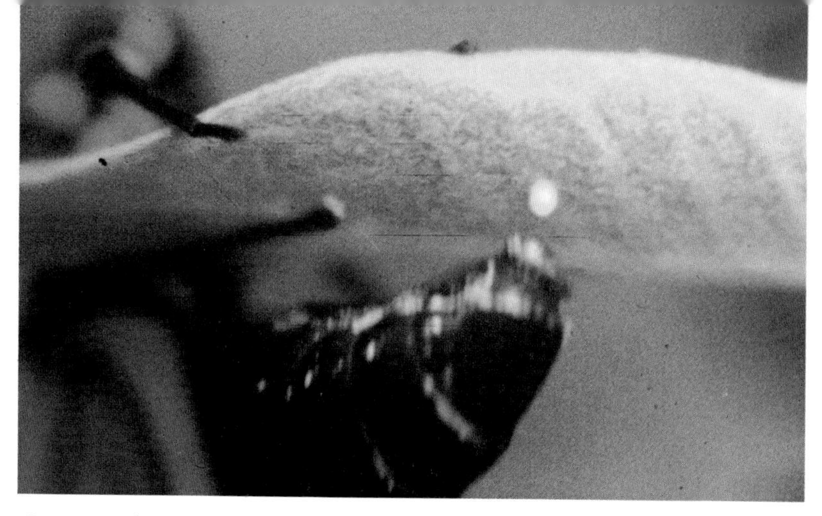

An egg being deposited from the tip of a female Monarch's abdomen

If you are lucky enough to see her flying from leaf to leaf, follow and observe. Once an egg is laid, her interest in it ends. And after all her hundreds of eggs are laid, her own life will fade away.

She may have flown thousands of miles and her fragile wings may be tattered and worn. Or she might be a young butterfly recently born on the northward migration route.

Usually she deposits only one egg under each leaf that she chooses. You will soon understand the advantage of that.

It helps to use a magnifying glass when examining the underside of the leaves because the egg is as small as the head of a pin. Magnified, you can see that it is cone-shaped, ribbed, and greenish white. Without a magnifying glass it's easy to mistake smooth round droplets of hardened milkweed juice for eggs. These will not hatch.

Cut at least one inch of the leaf surrounding the egg and bring it indoors, but not into an air-conditioned room.

THE INCUBATOR

To keep the piece of leaf fresh, place it on a moist paper towel in a tinfoil tray or on a plate. Use paper towels that have no chemical odor when wet.

A plastic bag wrapped around the tray also helps keep the leaf from drying out. A polyethylene bag is the only plastic we have found not harmful to caterpillars.

HATCHING

About four days after the egg was laid, or longer in a cool place, it is ready to hatch.

A black dot can now be seen at the tip

Left: Egg ready to hatch, greatly magnified

Middle: Eating his "eggshell"

Right: Eating another egg

of the egg. This is the head of the baby caterpillar.

Soon his head pokes through a hole he eats in his "eggshell" and gradually he eats his way out. (I say "he," but we can't tell male from female in this larval stage. To find out, we must wait for the butterfly.)

After the new-born caterpillar has made a first meal of his empty "shell," he would eat any eggs that were nearby, so it's good that the mother tends to lay her eggs on separate leaves.

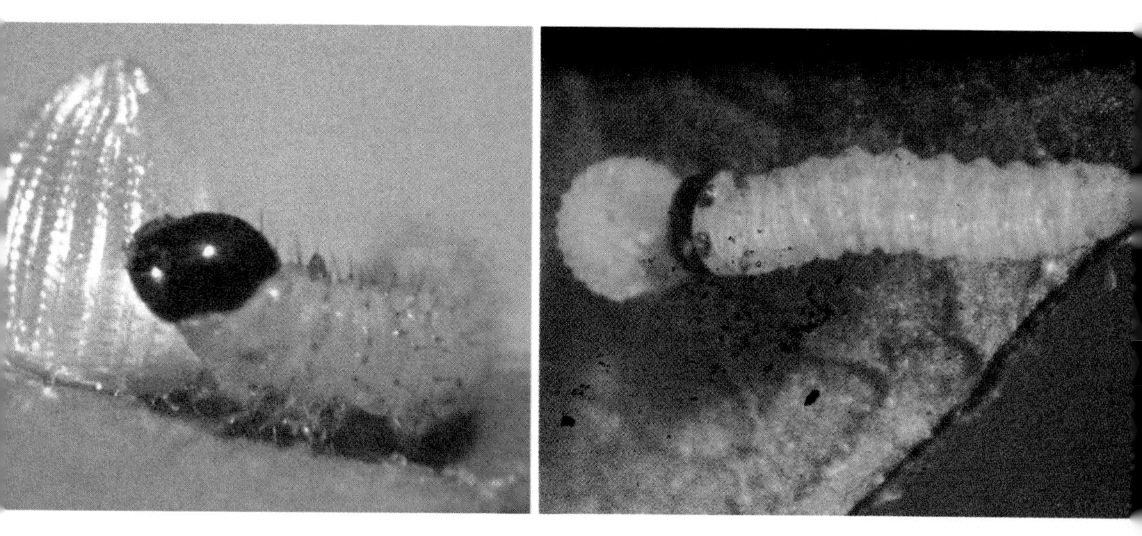

Next, the tiny caterpillar begins eating the soft part of the leaf, later nibbling small holes through it.

In a few days he has doubled his size. Now yellow, white, and black stripes ring his body. He spends all his time eating, resting, and eating some more. You have to keep him supplied with fresh milkweed leaves.

Left: Various sized caterpillars share milkweed leaves in an incubator tray. The girl is about to transfer a half-grown caterpillar to the large rearing cage (in background) where she is raising a few dozen Monarchs.

Puff the plastic bag to trap air inside. He doesn't need much. Air enters his body through a row of small holes along his sides, connected to tubes that deliver it to all his organs without the benefit of lungs.

After about a week in the incubator tray, the caterpillar is large enough to transfer to a rearing cage where he will have more room to move around and later go into the next stage of his metamorphosis.

THE REARING CAGE

Various types of rearing cages can accommodate a few Monarchs at a time. The most elaborate is one my naturalist husband developed, using four pieces of wood. A narrow jar of water holds a stem of milkweed leaves and is bound to the frame by a rubber band. A plastic bag, whose opening fits tightly around the

Overall size:
10″ H × 3″ W × 8¼″ L

base, keeps the caterpillar inside and the leaves from drying.

For those with less time or skill in carpentry, a jumbo-size glass jar will do very well, as many teachers have discovered. Inside, place a small jar of water tightly covered with a sandwich bag. Poke a hole to insert a stem of milkweed leaves. Or else, pour clean sand in the small jar and

insert the stem. Keep the sand wet but not enough to drown the caterpillar, should he fall in. Tie a double layer of gauze over the top of the jumbo jar.

Another type of cage is the cylinder made of fine screening about a foot high. Roll the screen so that the bottom fits into a large jar lid or the bottom inch of a big tin can. Tape the overlapping sides. A plate or tightly fitted plastic bag serves as a top.

Far left: Cylinder cage made of rolled screening
Left: Milk carton cage

If all else is unavailable, use a half-gallon milk carton. Simply cut out four side panels and the top. Inside, place a jar of milkweed leaves and the caterpillar, then lower the carton into a plastic bag and tie a double layer of gauze over the top.

Now you have a habitat which can support one, two, or three caterpillars. To raise more, you might make use of an empty aquarium covered by screening.

Change the milkweed leaves every other day or so. The caterpillar must eat enough to nourish himself now, and also in his next stage when he won't eat at all.

You will notice dark droppings that resemble peppercorns. This is the caterpillar's waste and can be removed when you change the leaves.

Full-grown caterpillar, about two inches long

If you see the caterpillar wriggling out of his skin, don't be alarmed. His skin doesn't grow larger as he grows. The tightness triggers a gland to release a slippery fluid between his old and new skins and he sheds the old. This is called *molting* and he will do it five times. After the fifth time he will no longer be a cater-pillar.

To prepare the cage for that remarkable event, place a twig in it with a horizontal branch as long as the space allows—from which he will be able to hang.

PREPARING FOR THE LAST MOLT

Having eaten for two weeks or more, the caterpillar is fully grown, about two inches long. Now he searches for a safe place to change into his pupal form. He must hang so that when he emerges as a butterfly, his wings will have room to expand without touching anything else.

He crawls around to find just the right spot. Although nearly blind, seeing only light through three simple eyes on each side of his head, he is able to feel his way around. As he moves, he spins a safety line of silk from a fine tube, called a *spinneret,* on his lower lip. This silk will be an important help as he attaches himself to the twig.

You will know he has selected his spot when he stops wandering.

After a while he weaves a tiny button of white silk and walks over it until the tip of his abdomen reaches it. Now he clamps his two rear legs into it. He seems in no hurry to end his caterpillar life.

Very slowly each of his remaining legs loosens its grip on the twig and lets go—four pairs of fleshy legs on his abdomen and three pairs of jointed legs in front. As the last support is gone, his body swings head down, suspended.

Already his caterpillar organs are dying, but out of that death will come his wonderful new life.

He hangs peacefully in a "J" position for a day and a night, his long black feelers limp.

Caterpillar in "J" position, greatly magnified

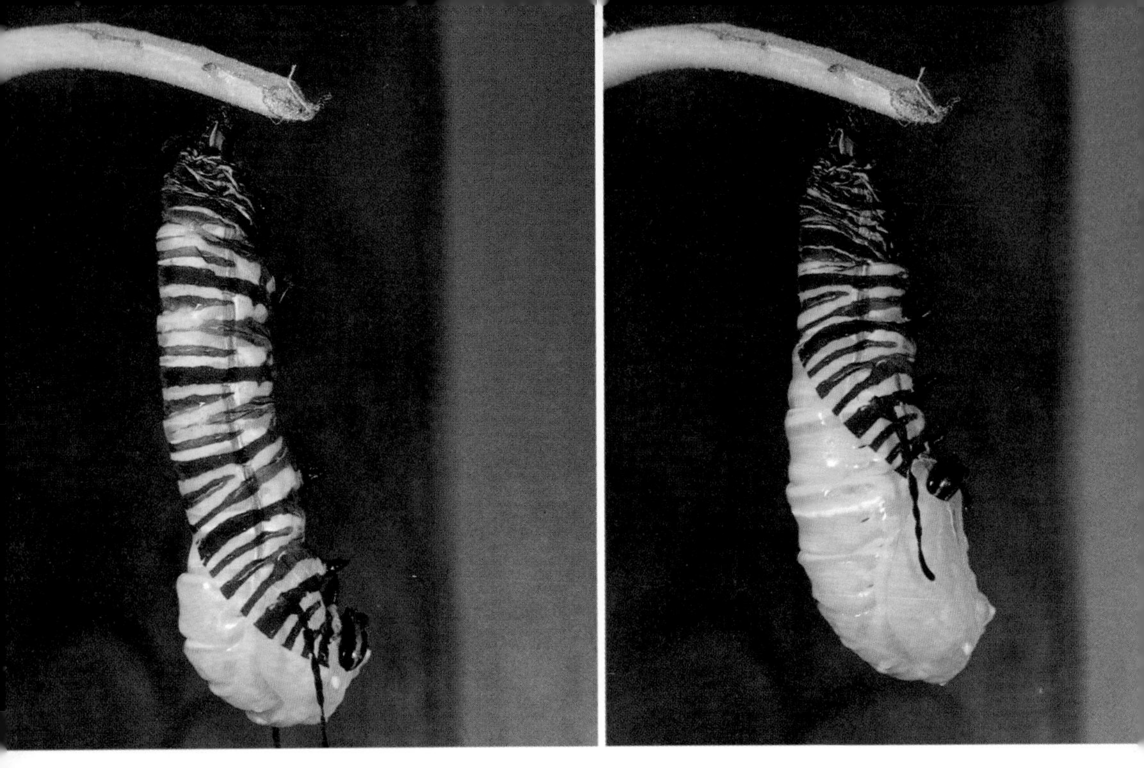

His skin rips up his back

BECOMING A CHRYSALIS

Finally he is ready to molt for the last time. Stretching himself again and again, he pushes the skin away from his head until it splits at the back of his neck and rips up his back. His rippling movements push his skin upward, and along with it, his face and legs. Underneath is a soft green blob.

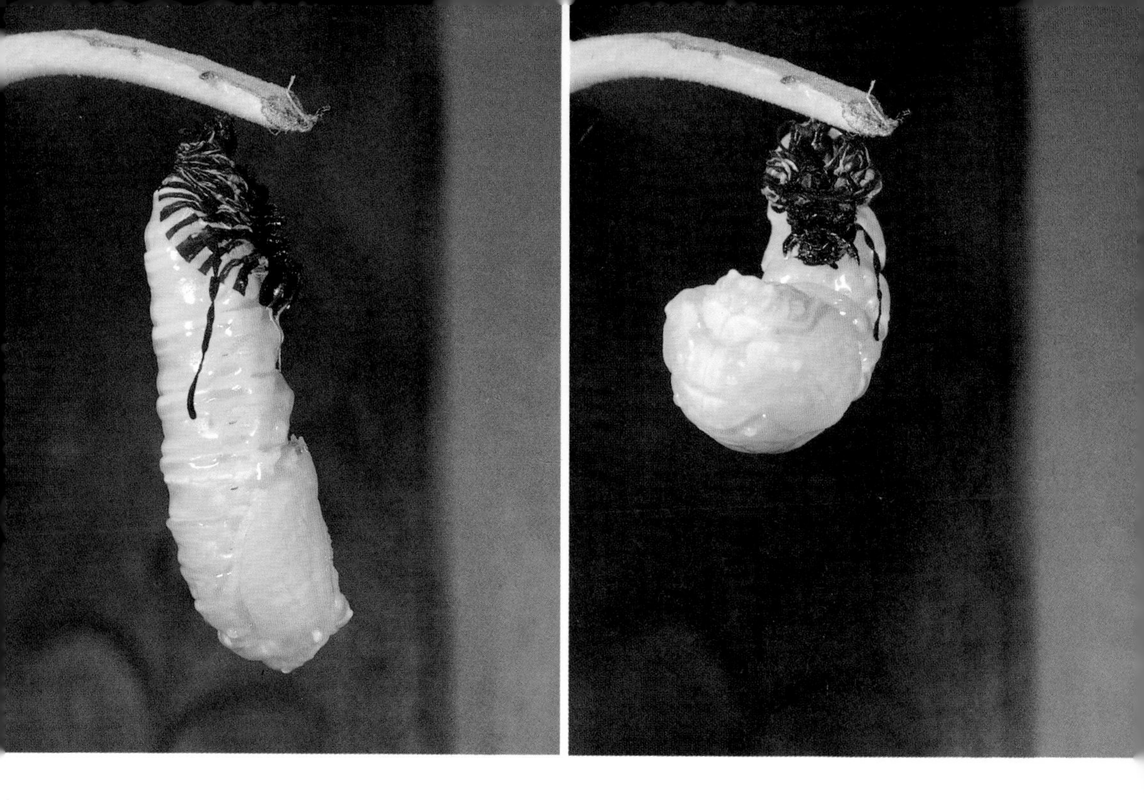

Right now he must work very hard. What happens in the next moment will tell whether he lives or not. Under his skin at the end of his abdomen is a shiny black stem called a *cremaster,* with microscopic hooks in it. He must hook this into the silk button, which he cannot see or feel, before throwing his skin away. If he can't do it, he will fall and die.

After successfully completing this difficult acrobatic feat, he twists until the cremaster is tightly hooked and his skin drops to the ground.

In an hour, the green blob becomes smooth and harder. In a few hours, little gold dots appear in the chrysalis. They aren't real gold, but they might fool almost anyone.

Yesterday he was a caterpillar and today he's a beautiful jade-green chrysalis, which, however, should not be handled.

A chrysalis is a butterfly *pupa.* Pupa means "doll," and an insect in this stage doesn't move. But, although he seems to be resting, many changes are going on. Butterfly cells were stored inside him from the time he formed within the egg. Now they begin to grow and multiply.

The chrysalis will hang for nine to fourteen days. His development is slower in cool places, faster in warm.

About one and a half days before the butterfly breaks out, you notice a change in the chrysalis from green to teal blue and a gradual darkening. Twelve hours later it becomes transparent enough to see orange wings.

THE BUTTERFLY BREAKS OUT

Soon the butterfly stirs and the chrysalis shell turns frosty here and there as he loosens himself from it.

He rests, then stirs again, and the shell cracks at its seams. He presses against it.

Suddenly it opens . . .

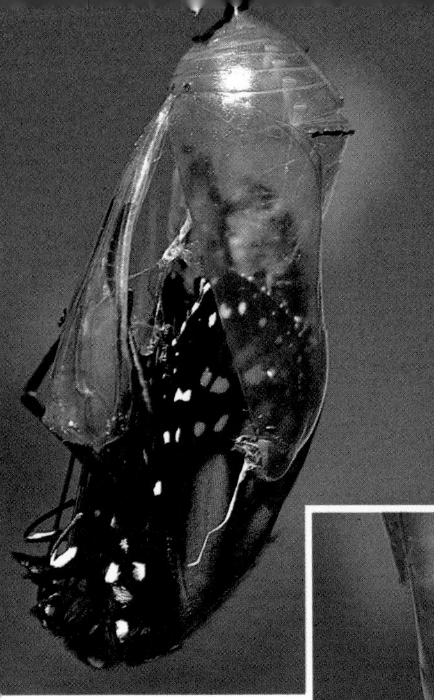

His abdomen tumbles out in a backward flip and the rest of him follows.

If you blink, you could miss this dramatic moment!

The butterfly clings to his empty chrysalis shell as his muscles pump blood into his soft, crinkled wings. Within eight minutes they expand to full size, but they are still damp and must dry before he can fly.

He coils and uncoils the two halves of his long sucking tube to match their notches and connect them into a single tube. Otherwise, he won't be able to drink.

For an hour or more he clings to his shell, clasping it with his long legs. He seems to have only two pairs of legs, but a smaller pair is folded in front.

As he waits, a few red-brown drops fall from the end of his abdomen. These are the wastes that were stored while he was a chrysalis.

When he opens his wings you can tell he is male by a small black dot on each hindwing, marking the male scent glands. Can you see that the top Monarch below is a male? The other butterflies are either females or their wings are folded, covering the males' black dots.

Release the butterfly outdoors the next morning unless it is raining. In that case, he might accept a sip of sugar water from a saucer to tide him over.

Outside, he'll circle in the air, fluttering higher to get his bearings. Monarchs that hatch in spring and mid-summer will mate and the females lay eggs, but those that hatch in late summer and autumn wait to mate and lay eggs until after winter. They are the ones that migrate south, finding refreshment stands of flowers along the way.

A butterfly sips the nectar of flowers the way you sip soda through a straw, but the "straw" is part of his or her mouth and is called a *proboscis.* Kept neatly coiled until needed, he extends it deep into flowers. Grains of pollen stick to it, rubbing off on the next flower he visits and fertilizing it, so that its seed can grow into new plants.

Thus, without knowing it, butterflies "pay" the flowers for their food by performing a necessary service—pollination. By raising butterflies, you are helping too.

ABOUT OTHER BUTTERFLIES

All butterfly species go through the same stages of metamorphosis, but their timing and behavior vary greatly. Some hibernate as caterpillars under wood or stone or in a leaf shelter. The hibernating chrysalides are held securely to twigs by silk loops. Adult butterflies that hibernate find shelter in rock crevices, loose bark, or hollow trees.

It might be difficult to raise a Great Spangled Fritillary because soon after hatching, the caterpillar hibernates all winter and in spring feeds on violets at night, hiding during the day. Black Swallowtails, however, are easy to raise and their eggs are not hard to find.

Black Swallowtail eggs are found on Queen Anne's lace.

RAISING A BLACK SWALLOWTAIL

You can recognize Black Swallowtails by the double row of yellow spots on their black wings, a row of blue spots on their hindwings, and the tails that give them their name.

The female lays smooth yellow eggs singly under the flowers of Queen Anne's lace, on the thin stems of their florets, and on parsley leaves and other plants of the carrot family.

Place the flower with its egg and leaves on several inches of wet sand in a jumbo-size glass jar tightly covered by gauze.

Four to ten days after the egg was laid, it hatches. The young caterpillar is dark with a white saddle mark, but as she (or he) grows and molts, yellow-dotted black bands appear on green skin.

Young Black Swallowtail caterpillars eating parsley

Full-grown Black Swallowtail caterpillar is almost two inches long.

If disturbed, she thrusts out an orange, forked organ that gives off an unpleasant odor.

Supplied with fresh leaves, the caterpillar eats for about two weeks. Before she is ready to become a chrysalis, add a straight stick as thick around as a fountain pen, stuck firmly into a jar of sand at a slight angle.

She will make a silk button on the stick and attach her hind legs to it. Then, it's fascinating to watch her standing upright, weaving a safety belt of many strands of silk to support herself before shedding her skin.

The next day, she splits the skin down her back. She must detach her rear end from the silk button—hanging for a second only by the safety belt—and bring her cremaster around the skin and fasten it into the silk button.

The chrysalis is pearly green or brown. In about twelve days the butterfly will emerge, unless it is late in the season and the chrysalis will winter over. Then, one spring day a Swallowtail will break out and climb upward, clinging to the stick while her lovely wings expand and dry.

The survival of butterflies is threatened when buildings replace meadows, and grounds are poisoned by weed-killers. But fortunately, more people are learning to leave some natural areas around their homes to welcome wildflowers and butterflies.

The eggs of these common butterflies are found on their larval food plants:

BUTTERFLY	LARVAL FOOD PLANTS
Regal Fritillary	Violets
Pearl Crescent	Asters (Eggs laid in clusters; larvae feed in group)
Mourning Cloak	Willow, poplar (Eggs laid in cluster; larvae feed in group)
Red Admiral	Nettles, hops (Larva makes silk shelter in leaf)
Painted Lady	Thistle (Larva makes shelter of leaf bits)
American Painted Lady	Everlastings (Larva makes shelter of leaf bits)
Buckeye	Plantain, gerardia
Viceroy	Willow, aspen, poplar
Giant Swallowtail	Citrus, prickly ash, rue
Tiger Swallowtail (Eastern)	Wild cherry, tulip tree (Larva makes shelter in rolled leaf)
Tiger Swallowtail (Western)	Willow, poplar, hops (Larva makes shelter in rolled leaf)
Spicebush Swallowtail	Sassafras, spicebush (Larva makes shelter in rolled leaf)
Anise Swallowtail	Anise, sweet fennel
Black Swallowtail	Queen Anne's lace, parsley
Monarch	Milkweed

Most butterflies have two generations a year in the north and more in the south. It is the last brood that hibernates over winter or migrates.

HIBERNATION AND MIGRATION

New-born caterpillar hibernates. Single brood.

Hibernates as part-grown caterpillar.

Butterfly hibernates, sometimes pupa.

Hibernates as butterfly or pupa. May become pupa in shelter.

Hibernates as butterfly or pupa. Sometimes migrates.

Hibernates as butterfly or pupa.

Hibernates as butterfly. Sometimes migrates.

Hibernates as part-grown caterpillar in shelter of silk and leaf.

Hibernates as pupa.

Hibernates as pupa.

Hibernates as pupa.

Hibernates as pupa.

Hibernates as pupa.

Hibernates as pupa.

Migrates

INDEX